New Boss, Same Chair

LaShawna Brown

NEW BOSS, SAME CHAIR

Printed in the United States of America

Published in Tulsa, Oklahoma, by LaShawna Brown.

Edited by Writing By Michele, LLC, Tulsa, OK

Cover art and interior design by Darby Harmon
www.DarbyHarmon.com

ISBN (print): 979-8-218-57211-2

ISBN (ebook): 979-8-218-57210-5

Dedication

Dear God, Shema.

To my amazing and hilarious husband for
always believing in and supporting me.

Introduction

Healing. It is not the word I expected to begin a book on leadership with. Yet that is the word God placed in my mind one morning. So, I asked, "Why healing?" The answer: Healing comes from doing, from being active in the process of moving forward and making progress. When you bring it down to basics, isn't that what leadership is all about? It is making progress when the playing field is not always smooth and easy.

My story of leadership originated from a place of brokenness; a workplace that had been disrupted by an abrupt exit. People were shaken, unsure, brokenhearted, betrayed, and needed healing. Often, a leader can help in that healing process. Certainly, the best leaders do. Great leaders provide stability, structure, and consistency as they bring a team together to accomplish a goal. Community is what a leader curates, and by doing so, healing begins.

Perhaps you walked, jumped, were pushed, or volunteered into a tough situation. Nothing like learning by fire, right? Maybe you are a seasoned leader and are going through an arduous season at work. We know everything is not always butterflies, unicorns, and rainbows. Yet your team needs you to help them through the mess and provide a safe, stable environment in which they, and the organization itself, can thrive.

Holding together a department after the abrupt exit of our director, who happened to be my mentor, and bringing healing to my team as well as myself — that was my first official leadership role. When I was asked to become the Interim Director in that challenging situation, the opportunity certainly was not presented as, "Hey, we need you to hold this department together." Yet that is exactly what happened. Our team came together as a community, worked through the storms, healed as a team, and came out stronger in the end.

This book is a guide to leading well regardless of the circumstances surrounding your entrance into leadership. Whether you are new to leadership or have been at this some time now, the five steps outlined in this book will ensure you are leading well through the ups and downs all businesses and industries inevitably face. Through these essential skills and principles, you can help provide healing, growth, and community to weather the storms.

As you continue your leadership journey, I encourage you to not stop learning with this book! New and complicated situations and opportunities will present themselves, and you will need to tap into more leadership learning and keep growing in your leadership skills. There are so many lessons to be learned in the difficult parts of being a leader; this one book cannot teach you everything you need to know, but it is a start. Each chapter within this book is designed to give you a foundation on which to build your leadership skills. At the end of each chapter, you will find a list of next steps, as well as various resources on how to dig deeper and learn more about the ideas shared in the chapter. You, too, can accomplish positive outcomes as you expand your leadership skills and learn to thrive in the position you are in. That is what this book is about.

You've got this! Let's get started.

Chapter 1
Healing

If you had asked me twelve years ago what my path to leadership and my role as a leader would be known for, the word 'healing' would not have been my catchphrase. Yet that is exactly what I have come to see leadership can be: a way forward to healing in an organization. In fact, like many who are thrust into leadership, I learned about leading and healing the hard way.

The Story

Friday afternoon, my cell rang. "Shawna, there were strange goings-on today at work," declared my colleague and friend.

That was an intriguing comment, considering we worked at a hospital, in the basement and right next to the morgue! What could be stranger than all the weirdness of working at your desk while hearing a groan coming from the next room where there should be silence?

"Dude, no one talks like that! What do you mean?" I asked.

"The human resources lady and security followed our boss around this afternoon. They put a stack of papers and checks on your desk, and then they walked her out of the office."

My stomach dropped. *What did she do?* I wondered, *Who is going to lead us now?* And then the realization hit me: When I walked in on Monday, they were going to ask me to lead our department. Why else would they put stuff on my desk? Why wouldn't they have handed the paperwork over to one of my co-workers?

Holy cow, Batman!

Immediately, questions and concerns began rolling through my mind, and there were a lot of them. Could I do this? Could I step into my boss's role? At the time, my husband and I had three young kids. What would this change of position do to our family? Did I have enough time in my day to carry out a change like this, lead a department, and also have enough time for my family? Could our marriage endure the stress? Could I manage the stress? Did I even know enough to lead? What did my boss even do other than go to meetings? Was this the next step in my career?

I wrestled with worries like these all weekend. I talked over the situation with a trusted friend. She listened, asked great questions, encouraged and supported me in prayer to make the right decision, whatever that might be.

Sunday morning while I was serving at church, the Chief of Staff at my hospital walked in. We were both shocked to see each other. We chatted about church and which campus he usually attends — which was not the same one I attended. As it turned out, he had come to my location the Sunday after that strange phone call to check out our band, a one-off situation. There was no mention of the hospital or work at all. Was this coincidence or God's perfect timing? I knew it was a God-wink telling me to take the next step. Scary as it might be and unprepared as I thought I was, I knew what my answer would be on Monday.

Monday morning began like normal: wake up early, get the kids ready, drop them off at daycare, head to the office. In the car, I said a prayer that became my daily prayer as a leader: "Lord, let me accomplish what You need me to accomplish today.

And please do not let me screw up any of Your plans! Amen!" Real and simple.

Arriving at the office, the buzz was all around. Our Vice President asked me to gather the team for a nine-a.m. meeting. I immediately got on it.

We gathered together as requested, and our Vice President and the Chief of Staff from Sunday's surprise run-in addressed the team. They relayed that our director had been let go. Our minds were reeling, and there was just silence as we sat there in shock, taking in the announcement.

They stated that additional information regarding our department's leadership would be forthcoming, then we were dismissed. I was asked to speak privately with the Vice President and the Chief of Staff. They asked if I knew the circumstances around my boss's dismissal. I relayed I only knew what they had just told us. Then the moment I had been contemplating all weekend happened.

"We would like you to step in as Interim Director until we can find a replacement."

There was a sense of loyalty to the company, the doctors, and my teammates that drove me to accept the Interim Director position. If not me, then who would the company bring in? How would an outsider lead? Would they try to overhaul the whole department? What if they were horrible and did not fit the culture of our team? In my heart, those were not chances I could put our team through. I wanted to retire from this company and already had put in thirteen years.

"Certainly," I said. "I am up for the task."

I am one of those "whatever is needed, I will get it done" kind of people. In my mind I was certain I could still do my normal job and the Interim Director job, no problem. Oh, how naive and wrong I was.

And so began my leadership journey. I quickly realized I knew nothing about leadership! I knew how to be a dependable employee, get my work done, be a team player, and do what I was asked to do. But I did not know a single thing about heading up a team. It left me thinking, "Now what?"

I had no short, simple, "here is what you need to know" kind of book. A game plan? My game plan was survival! Remember my prayer? *Please do not let me screw it up*! I did not have time to digest every single John Maxwell book, listen to every podcast, or read a 400-page *For Dummies* book.

How About You?

How did you come into being the boss? Was it complicated, awkward, or chaotic? Maybe you stepped into it knowing what lay ahead. Maybe you were asked to fill in. Maybe you were hired after someone was fired. Many times, you are walking into a difficult and uneasy situation. How do you lead a hurting, reeling, or troubled team?

However you came into leadership, there are five steps I have learned that can help you and your team be successful. This book outlines these five steps and explores some of the nuances of each. You've got work to do now! This is a guide to hit the ground running for new leaders. It shouldn't be the last leadership book you read because we can all keep learning and growing. Yet this is a good place to start!

My hope is this book of five steps gives you the base you need to pull together a game plan and execute. Why five? I have a friend who will not even attempt a recipe if it has more than five ingredients. I do not want you to miss something that could help because it is too long or complicated.

You could have a million what-if's, what should I do's, and where do I start's running through your brain. Stop, breathe in and breathe out. One step at a time. You will not be able to download into your brain the leadership mastery of John Maxwell in a single day or weekend. Remember the Chinese proverb, "A journey of a thousand miles begins with a single step." This book is your start, your first, or even your next step. You are building a base armory of tools to face the leadership challenges in front of you.

In the following chapters, we are going to explore these five steps:

1. Know your team.

2. Know the rules.

3. Know how to communicate.

4. Know your role and expectations.

5. Execute with confidence and precision.

Are you ready? Let's go!

Your Next Steps

1. Identify 2-3 leaders who have influenced you and write down what you appreciated most about their leadership.

2. Take time to define why you want to lead.

3. How do you want to be known as a leader?

4. Turn the page and dive into Step 1 – Know Your Team.

Chapter 2
Know Your Team

People are all different — meaning they have different personalities, problems, experiences, backgrounds, work ethics, reliability, and just about anything else you can think of. It does not matter whether you hired them, or you inherited them — they are your team. You are working with them, and you need to know them.

Getting to know someone takes time. What are the benefits to investing the time to get to know your team? Knowing your team can help you when you are:

- Assigning tasks — You know the skillsets, strengths, and goals of each person and can assign tasks accordingly.

- Attempting to find solutions — You know who can invent solutions, who can discern whether possible solutions will work, and who can carry out solutions. Your team is more agile to pivot and change as needed.

- Building community — They feel known, part of a community, a valuable contributing member of something bigger than themselves. They do not feel alone when problems or obstacles arise.

- Communicating — Knowing how they best receive feedback, learn, and process information leads to clearer instructions, candid and to-the-point conversations, and faster response time to call-to-actions.

Build Connections to Strengthen Teams

"The most important single ingredient is knowing how to get along with people."

Theodore Roosevelt

Getting along with people in the workplace starts with understanding what drives them. *Harvard*

Business Review says the three things employees really want are career, community, and cause.[1]

- Career: This includes finding ways to help people use their strengths at work. This gives them more autonomy and control over their career. As leaders, we can promote our team's learning and development, so they are not staying stagnant.

- Community: Employees value feeling respected, cared about, and recognized by others. This desire drives our sense of connection and belongingness. As leaders, we can be intentional about how we create an atmosphere of respect and appreciation.

- Cause: This need is rooted in a sense of purpose. It involves making a meaningful impact, identifying with the organization's mission, believing that it does some good in the world. Employees want their career to be a source of pride.

---

[1] (Goler, Gale, Harrington, & Grant, 2018)

These three things make up the psychological contract, by which I mean the unwritten expectations and obligations between employees and employers. We may not officially sign anything, but we all expect and hope for these elements in every relationship, and work is no different. We are all looking to find a what, a who, and a why. In the workplace, this translates to a career, community, and purpose. When this unspoken social contract is fulfilled, employees bring their whole selves to work. But when it is breached, people become dissatisfied and less committed. They contribute less. They perform worse. So, these needs must be intentionally addressed if we want our team to succeed.

Patrick Lencioni in his book *The Five Dysfunctions of a Team* outlines a pyramid of what is necessary for a cohesive team. Think of Maslow's hierarchy of needs for the modern workplace. The foundation is Trust, then comes Conflict, Commitment, Accountability, and Results tops off the pyramid. Successful teams have a foundation of trust, are not afraid to disagree on ideas, are committed to the cause, hold each other accountable, and pay attention to results. When a team lacks one of these elements, it is identified as a dysfunction and should be addressed. We will look at an example later in this chapter.

Intentional Leadership Fosters Employee Satisfaction

A good leader will help employees find career, community, and cause in the workplace. My first job was at Video Network in the small town of Coweta, OK. By small, I mean we had three stoplights in the whole town when I was in high school. Shirley was the owner and manager of the video store. She took a chance on a fifteen-year-old girl who walked in one afternoon and asked if she was hiring.

Shirley was my first example of a great leader. She knew her employees, taking an interest in how we performed in school and what extracurricular activities we had. Our relationships with her and her knowledge of us on a personal level came as a culmination of regular conversations over days, weeks, months.

Looking back, these conversations helped her know what our priorities were and how often she should schedule us to work and which days/nights would be best. She learned what our skills were as she worked alongside us. Were we good with customers, friendly, accurate in data entry as we checked in movies and checked people out? Could we upsell candy, pop, popcorn, video games? Did we treat everyone with the same respect and attention? Did we follow directions?

Shirley also never asked us to do anything she was not willing to do. Cleaning the shelves was the dreaded task. One afternoon I walked in and she said, "Shawn-Shawn, I cleaned the horror section because I know you are too scared to look at the boxes. I need you to clean the action section." She knew me! You know, I cleaned the action section and went on to clean the drama section as well that day. When your team feels known, they will do more than you ask and will exceed your expectations.

Shirley also introduced me to Black Friday shopping. She invited her employees to come along if they wanted. Oh, what an adventure it was! We went to K-Mart, and Shirley's goal was to grab a stereo for her grandson. Shirley was probably in her fifties at the time; she only had one lung and was tiny in stature. So, sixteen-year-old me was her muscle, which was hilarious because I was not much taller than she was! The hunt for the stereo was on. Once we had secured the gift in Shirley's cart, I knew Black Friday was my new tradition. For the next five years or so, our little crew of shoppers, led by the fearless Shirley, went shopping on Black Friday.

Shirley was involved in the local community as well, donating rentals for raffles, letting us sell our candy bars for band and choir at the store, serving as a member of the Chamber of Commerce, and loving when the Fall Festival shut down Main Street and planted itself right outside the storefront. One would think the Fall Festival shutting down the main entrance to your store would be frustrating to a business owner. Oh no, it was an opportunity to see even more people in the town. Shirley never stated what our mission was at the video store, yet it was evident when you watched her. Our mission was to be a part of the community, to be kind to people and help their day to be a little better or a little more entertaining, to put a smile on as many faces as possible, and to share the light and love that was inside of us.

I never resigned from the video store. I still have a key to the door even though it changed owners and closed many years ago. Shirley passed away over a decade ago, and I still visit her grave. She made such an impact on so many young lives within the walls of her little video store. Shirley is who I want to be as a leader. I was just looking for a job at fifteen years old. What Shirley gave me instead:

- The foundation to a career I would not step into until decades later.

- A sense of community within the walls of the video store.

- A purpose to bring light and joy to anyone who walked into our video store.

Just like Shirley did, your goal is to know what your employees are looking for in their career, create a community culture where employees can thrive, and give employees a cause they can believe in and work toward. Let's tackle getting to know your team next.

Team Groups

Organizations have many levels, and to be successful they all need to work together. You have a lot of people on your team. Breaking them up, there are four basic groups. With each group, you will approach communication, problem-solving, and decision-making differently. To be a good leader, you need to know these groups and how to navigate the nuances of each.

Direct Reports

As the name implies, these are the people who report directly to you. You sign off on their timecards, performance evaluations, paid time off requests, and day to day oversight.

Teams/Departments Reporting to You

Depending on your leadership position and the organizational structure of the company, you may have several teams or departments within the company that report up to you. For example, you may have a supervisor, manager, or director that reports directly to you, and they have their own set of direct reports. That team reports through their leader to you.

Other Departments

There are departments you and your department(s) collaborate with frequently to accomplish tasks, goals, and objectives. Examples include legal, quality, marketing, contracting, shipping and receiving to name a few.

Your Leadership

Who you report to is a key part of your team. Think about who you report to and who they report to, all the way up to the CEO/President, as your leadership.

Direct Reports

You know your direct reports' names, but you need to know them as a person and as an employee, including their aspirations, strengths, weaknesses, and most of all how to communicate with them! I know that is a lot. You will not get it all in one session. This takes time. You are building a foundation of knowledge and trust.

Where in the world do you begin? With a one-on-one meeting, low key, not formal, maybe a coffee. My favorite offices have a seating area separate from the desk. This is where a casual conversation can happen. Try to make the one-on-one feel a bit more relaxed. Have a notebook to jot down things you would like to remember. Have some questions or prompts prepared to help learn about them. Here are some I have used.

- Tell me about you. Are you from here? How long have you lived here? What is your favorite food, drink, or snack?

- Tell me what your role here encompasses. What do you like best about your job? What do you like least?

- If you have done a personality profile in the past, can you share which one and what the results were?

- What do you want to accomplish in your career here?

- What do you want me to know? This question may seem a little open-ended or vague, but there is a purpose. In 2018 during the trial of former Olympic doctor, Lawrence G. Nassar, the number of victims willing to testify was low. It is terrifying to publicly tell your story. However, Judge Rosemarie Aquilina was presiding over the trial and asked a simple, yet profound question: "What would you like me to know?" It was not an interrogation; it was an opportunity for them to tell what they thought was important and pertinent. By asking this question, the number of testimonies almost doubled. Asking this question helps you learn what they see as important, their values, their concerns.

- Do you have any questions for me? Remember, this is a conversation, not a quiz. When you have something in common, chat for a moment about it. You are not only learning about them, but they are also learning about you.

It is imperative that you have these one-on-one meetings with your direct reports and the leader of the teams or departments that report to you. Take notes or if that feels awkward in the moment, take a few minutes after your meeting and write down the key takeaways so you can reference them later. If you have a large team, you will not be able to remember all the details from every person. Keeping a record to reflect on and refer to later is helpful.

Teams and Departments Reporting to You

You may or may not be able to have the "one-on-one get to know you" meetings with each member of the teams/departments that report to you if there is a leader between you and the employees. There are other ways to get to know the teams/departments that report to you; consider luncheons to celebrate holidays, birthdays, or milestones. This not only helps you get to know your team but provides an opportunity for your team to know each other. When we know more about our team members and their lives, they become teammates, not just people who we walk by each day and occasionally speak to. They become partners in pursuing and accomplishing the goals and tasks assigned to the team. In the transition from team member to teammate, the team begins to understand each other's personalities, drive, and struggles, which leads to more grace and understanding in the workplace.

What does understanding have to do with the workplace? Simply stated: culture. The culture of a team defines how they treat each other. A culture that encourages grace and understanding for each other is one that fosters innovation, community, clear communication, personal growth, and the It factor. No, not the Stephen King novel *It*. More like *It: How Churches and Leaders Can Get It and Keep It* by Craig Groeschel.

Have you ever walked into a restaurant, store, business, church, or group gathering and there was this something that made the place somewhere you wanted to be or something you wanted to be involved in? You could not really explain what *it* was that made you feel like that; there was a sense, mood, vibe, something that felt like this place/group had *it*. That is the It factor. When people understand, know, and care for each other, the It factor intensifies. Create a culture that fosters less negative friction between people and watch how much your team will accomplish.

Other Departments

Figure out who these other departments are that you will need to collaborate with; and be the one who takes that first step to connect with them. Your leader should be able to help you identify them. You may also have gleaned some insights from your own direct reports and department leaders. Ask the department leader to lunch and see if you can slip some of the questions in. At minimum, ask:

- Tell me about you.

- How do our teams collaborate?

- Do you see opportunities where we could improve collaboration?

To build some trust, see if the suggestion for improved collaboration is feasible. I am not suggesting you make changes immediately — especially since making changes immediately after becoming a leader can create stress on your staff. But if the requested improvement is something that can be done in the next few months, see if you or your team can make it happen.

Here is an example of what it can look like to collaborate well with a different department:

The Quality Assessment Department (QA) at the hospital had standing meetings with the doctors to review quality of care cases within their specialty. The QA Nurses mentioned that they were coming to 7 a.m. meetings or staying for 5 p.m. meetings, but no one was showing up. They had to do a lot of preparation for the meetings, especially to have no one to show up. The nurses were no doubt frustrated to have wasted their time preparing for a meeting that did not happen.

Our department was already reaching out and reminding the physicians of the meetings. So, we made a simple change to the phone call; we asked for confirmation they would be attending the meeting. With this information, we were able to tell the QA Nurses 1-2 days before the meeting who would be attending. They could then adjust the cases they pulled and how many accordingly, or they would know that the meeting could be cancelled. This built trust between our departments and streamlined processes for the QA Department.

At another time, we worked with the Quality Department who reviewed complaints and concerns submitted regarding providers. For years and years, my team would get a paper copy of the Quality Department's review and we would place them in the provider's paper file. When our teams began to work remotely, we had to figure out how to move this paper-based process to an electronic one. We collaborated, found they already track this information on a spreadsheet, and were able to share the necessary information in a secure fashion electronically that both departments could access when necessary. This change saved a substantial amount of time for my team in tracking down and searching for paper copies of the complaints and concerns.

Let's elaborate on the approach to making these changes happen. Take the idea back to your direct reports or department, whomever it would involve or effect, and ask for their thoughts. Getting buy-in from the team is important. If they feel they have had an opportunity to discuss and express their opinions, thoughts, and ideas, they will better support the change. We do not want to be the new sheriff in town making radical changes. We want to be a helpful partner, one who is trying to remove pebbles from our shoes.

Pebbles & Boulders

Have you ever had a pebble in your shoe? Sure, you can walk, but that minuscule pebble seems like a boulder when trying to walk. Your steps can be off, slower than normal, perhaps even hindered in overall distance. Sweet relief occurs once the pebble is removed. Surprisingly, there is also a renewed energy, that optimism when something better appears, and our steps become more assertive, purposeful, and faster. When working through ideas, possible solutions, issues and problems, think of them in terms of pebbles and boulders to help figure out the approach to take.

Pebbles – These are the small tweaks that can be made to make work or processes flow better and easier for your team, like the example earlier in the chapter of the Quality Department sharing the complaints and concerns documentation. We could still get the job done using the paper process; however, the spreadsheet was a small tweak on something they were already doing. Simply bringing up and talking about possible ways to help each other brought about a smoother process and removed a pebble from both of our shoes.

Boulders – These are issues, struggles, or hindrances to your team that will take time and energy to alleviate. They cannot be resolved without effort, but the effort will be worth it.

Here is an example of a boulder we have tackled over the past year.

In Patrick Lencioni's *Five Dysfunctions of a Team*, he shares a parable of a new leader coming in and assessing where the team is and who should stay and who should go. When I read this book, I knew I needed to assess my team and address the dysfunctions we had. It was exciting and tremendously scary. We called it Team Cultivation. Yes, it was team building, but you know no one wants to do a trust fall, and that is the first thing that comes to mind when you say team building.

I read the book, had our team answer the assessment questions, and compared their responses to my assessment of the team. Our dysfunctions were in the areas of Trust and Absence of Conflict. I used the resources in the book to map out a game plan to address the issues and cultivate our team into a trusting one that was not afraid to have conflicting ideas, leading to productive conversations and good decisions.

I would like to say that was easy and took just a few days. Instead, it took planning and discussion with other trusted leaders. It was also assigned as a personal goal for each team member to meaningfully participate; it would be included in performance evaluations. What?! You mean my team was not jumping to be first in line to go through this exercise? They had to have it tied to their annual performance evaluation? I even knew it had to happen, and I was scared!

Together, we powered through. We got to know each other better and trust began to build. We developed and agreed on how we were to behave and that we were each going to be held accountable for our behavior and productivity. I know that sounds like a no-brainer, but there are times you inherit some team members who do not play by the same rules. We had conflict that was productive. I had difficult conversations with employees addressing behavior and/or productivity. Slowly, each person realized the team dynamic was changing, and the old ways were not acceptable anymore. By the end of that year, several team members moved on from our company. The team that remained is by far the most trusting, productive, accountable, and caring team I have ever been a part of.

Okay, back to how to do this. Start with the small things, the pebbles. They are usually minor and easily fixable. Small wins start the momentum of trust building. You need the team to trust you to tackle boulders together. Once you have spoken with your direct team, reach out to the other department/team leader and share the idea. If plausible, have them identify someone from their team who could collaborate to implement the idea.

Even beginning the collaboration starts to build trust between the teams and with you. To continue to build upon that trust, keep following through. Ensure the idea does not fall to the wayside. In other words, do not drop the ball. All those meetings are going to pile up, timecards are going to be due yet again, new pebbles and boulders will surface, and you may feel the task is too daunting. Be encouraged and do not lose sight of the goal! Set aside time on a regular basis to work on or check in on the collaboration. If you let the ball drop, the trust will fade. Yet, when the collaboration idea is complete and improvements are made, trust grows just a little more. Great job!

Your Leadership

Getting to know who you report to can be tricky. You do not want to be pushy, intrusive, or demanding. Come at it from the position that you are inquisitive and thirsty for their knowledge and expertise. This is not a time to tell your life story and they tell you theirs. Likely, you will be asking the questions and listening, not telling all about you. They will ask questions as they see appropriate.

You will likely have a scheduled ongoing one-on-one meeting with your direct leader. Use that time to ask questions. Here is a list to get started.

- Through your job interview, you may have gleaned a little information about them. If not, ask how long they have worked in the company and what led them there.

- What is their why for working here?

- What is the scope of their oversight within the organization?

- What is the most challenging part of their job?

- What is the most rewarding part of their job?

- What can you do to support them?

- What are their expectations of you?

- What is coming within the next one to five years at the company that they are excited about?

You may have more than one leader to whom you report; imagine the dotted line in the organizational chart. Have a similar conversation with them. Ask for a lunch meeting and pick out some of the previously mentioned questions like how you can support them, expectations, and ways they collaborate with the other leader(s) to whom you report.

When I worked at the hospital, the Director position supported the Medical Staff Leadership and was employed by the Hospital. There were times when these two groups disagreed, and the Director was left in the middle of the disagreement. What happens then? The Director provides support and expertise and attempts to navigate to a Third Alternative. Stephen Covey introduces the Third Alternative concept in his book, *The 7 Habits of Highly Effective People*. Essentially, it is an innovative decision that everyone can agree upon.

What does that look like in practice? Here is an example.

One year, the hospital administration wanted to bring in a residency program. This endeavor would mean a change in how the Medical Staff provided oversight of the attending physicians to the program to ensure patient safety. There had been a long history of turf battles over the privileges and oversight of these physicians to perform at a level the Medical Staff held to be appropriate and safe for patients. Together with representatives from administration, the Medical Staff, and the incoming attending physicians, a third alternative was formulated. It did not happen in one meeting. It took several meetings, over several months, to ensure everyone was agreeable and patient safety was not compromised. My role was to support the Administration and the Medical Staff. I did this by:

- Coordinating meetings by scheduling the room and reminding the attendees of the meetings.

- Inquiring what information, documentation, support, or research each group required for each meeting and delivering it prior to the meeting.

- Documenting the discussion, decisions, and action items of each meeting.

- Following up on action items to ensure they were completed in the timeframes set.

- Providing expertise when requested.

In the end the residency program was onboarded along with the attending physician group, in the timeframe administration requested and with the appropriate safety measures approved by the Medical Staff.

Leading Up

Just as people have different personality types, leaders have varied leadership styles. If you find yourself at odds with the leadership style of your boss, continue to do what is right, what is best. I am not suggesting that you defy direct orders. I am saying continue to be a positive role model, suggest ideas, consistently show up, and execute your tasks to the best of your ability. Be the best leader you can be, and model what a good leader is to those who report to you, and also to those who organizationally rank higher than you.

When I am new to a role or company, I take a back seat and observe. Observe the personalities, preferences, and body language of the whole team. I do not come in with an "I know everything" attitude or an "I deserve respect and attention" mindset. It is not my style, and I think that particular attitude and mindset can put off a lot of people. These are people you will need on your team and on your side.

When I entered a new role, I did not sit at the table when the entire department would all pile into a large conference room. The department consisted of roughly thirty individuals, which included one director and four managers. There were about twenty chairs at the table and benches that lined two walls. I sat at the back of the room, on a bench with the majority of my team. I had not yet proven myself to have a seat at the table. Your actions speak more than your title.

One goal that I set for myself: learn more about business. In reviewing and proposing my goals to my boss, I asked if I could read *Business Made Simple* by Donald Miller. My boss took the idea and made a goal for our department's leadership team to read and discuss the book together. We shared the simple and short videos in our weekly department staff meeting. The leadership book club continued on for many years and grew to include leaders from other departments.

At the end of the day, you have a lot of meetings to attend to get to know your team. It can feel overwhelming and cost time; the downstream reward of knowing them is well worth it. Remember the psychological contract? You need to know what makes them tick so you can fulfill your end of the contract.

Additional Reading List

It: How Churches and Leaders Can Get It and Keep It — Craig Groeschel

Leadership Secrets of Santa Claus — Eric Harvey
Start with Why — Simon Sinek

The Five Dysfunctions of a Team — Patrick Lencioni

<u>Your Next Steps</u>

1. Identify all of your direct reports and schedule a one-on-one meeting to ask the questions in the Direct Reports section.

2. Identify all the teams/departments that report to you, and schedule a luncheon to get to know them a little better. It can be as little as thirty minutes and can be a virtual bring your own lunch. Have a topic to break the ice (i.e., favorite summer memory, best Halloween costume, favorite recipe), but let the conversation flow.

3. Identify one department you will work with closely; schedule a meeting with the

department leader and ask the questions in the Other Departments section.

Chapter 3
Know the Rules

He watched his wife carefully trim the ends off the ham as she prepared to put it in the oven for supper, something he had seen her do for years.

"Honey, why do you cut the ends off the ham?" he asked.

"That is the way my mom and grandma both prepared their hams," she said.

Interesting, he thought as his wife finished putting the ham in the oven.

Although the conversation ended, the question lingered in her mind: *Why do we cut off the ends?* She decided to call her father to see if he knew. Her mother had passed some years ago.

"Dad, why did Mom and Grandma cut off the ends of the ham?"

After a thoughtful pause he responded, "Your Grandma's pan was too small for the ham. She had to trim it down to fit!"

The Value of Knowing the Rules

People and organizations all operate by rules. To play the game, you have got to know the rules. Thorough knowledge, understanding, and application of the rules is essential to your success as a leader. The rules are there as boundaries to know how far you are able to go and still be safe, compliant and legal. It is like seeing the speed limit sign and deciding to exceed the limit. Sure, you could speed, but you are taking a risk if you do. And at the leadership level, the risks have higher consequences than just a speeding ticket. Boundaries, therefore, are safeguards to potentially high consequences.

The best boundaries illustration I have come across is the story of a playground.

There was a nice new playground built right next to a busy street. The city would stop by and check on the playground. One day, they noticed there were not many kids playing and those who were there were huddled mostly in the middle of the playground. After gathering input from parents and others close to the playground location, they found the kids played in the middle because there was not anything between them and the danger of the busy street. The parents had created a boundary with their instructions, and the children had obeyed the boundary because they wanted to feel safe.

With this new information, the city built a chain-link fence around the playground. Quickly, the kids began playing all over the playground. In addition, the number of kids coming to play increased. Why did the fence help so much? The kids knew exactly how far they could play and still be safe. The fence created the boundaries they needed to be secure and have fun. As a result, the entire playground became much more enjoyable and better utilized.

That same sense of clear boundaries helps teams and organizations be more productive too. And as a leader, you get to help with that.

Red Rules and Blue Rules

As you think of rules, realize that it helps to know which are set in stone, and which you may have the ability to change or influence. I call this separating the red rules from the blue rules. Red rules are the laws, regulations, the speed limit; things you cannot change or do not control. Blue rules are like cutting the ends off the ham because that is the way we were taught or the way we have always done it. They are comfortable, they are established, but they can often be changed or tweaked.

Every industry has a set of rules, both red ones and blue ones. Do you know the rules of your industry? To name a few examples, we are talking about:

- Employment laws

- Tax laws

- Regulatory standards

- Company bylaws

- Company policies

Whether you are new to your company, industry, or trade or are a seasoned veteran, learn the rules. Those boundaries are going to help you and your team succeed. How exactly do you learn the rules? Ask! Is there a compliance department at your company? They will certainly know. Legal department? They know. Ask others on your team, like your boss, to direct you to internal sources that spell out or offer training in the rules and boundaries that your industry and organization adheres to.

When I first began working at the hospital, I was the receptionist. I scheduled meeting rooms, answered the phone, gave messages to co-workers, called physicians to remind them of upcoming meetings, and sent out the mailouts. I was required to follow the hospital Human Resources rules as an employee. Since I was reminding physicians of their meeting attendance, I also knew a few attendance requirements that were outlined in the Medical Staff Bylaws. Pretty simple.

When I transitioned to the role of a Credentialing Specialist, I learned a whole new set of rules, regulations, policies, procedures, and all of those Medical Staff Bylaws. With new responsibilities and job duties, the list of Red Rules I was required to know increased.

Then, when I stepped into the Interim Director position, the Red Rules increased yet again. I had to learn about employment laws, accreditation compliance, State Health Department surveys, and the list kept growing. When you step into leadership, even within the same industry, ensure you are gathering all of the next level rules you are required to know and follow.

Want some additional ways to gather those next level rules? Look for local, state, and national associations within your industry related to your area. Become a member, and then subscribe to the newsletter, publications, and emails they offer. Go to conferences, webinars, online trainings, and network with others in your field.

Through the process of researching and gathering the rules, you will be able to discern the Red Rules from the Blue Rules. This discernment will help when tackling those pebbles and boulders we learned about earlier. The team, boss, and other departments are all looking to see if you are going to make any changes, address issues that are brought to your attention, and create improvements. To make impactful innovations, you must know what can and cannot be altered. As the leader, you do not want to initiate adjustments that unknowingly go against the Red Rules and later must be undone. Knowing the rules is key to successful transformation as well as keeping you, your team, and your company in compliance.

Set Up a System to Keep Track of the Rules

As you gather these resources that outline the Red Rules, save them! Electronically saving them for an easy, searchable reference is standard. While using these resources, you may notice you access some more frequently than others. For those documents that you need regular and easy access to, I recommend a binder or notebook. What?! Yes, I am talking old-school printing documents to paper, using a three-hole punch, tabs to organize, and putting them together in a three-ring binder. I lovingly call it my Handy Dandy Notebook. For those of you who remember *Blue's Clues*, you may recognize the name of my notebook.

The notebook method has served me well over the years (and even continues to do so today). That first notebook in my first leadership role saved me so many times. When the Chief Medical Officer or Hospital President walked into my office with a question, the Notebook often held the information they needed. Seeing it on paper, holding it in their hands had its benefits. The notebook went with me to meetings for easy access when questions were raised as to whether or not this or that could be done legally.

This is true even today. A quick copy can be made of the page other leaders or employees need. They can make notes on it. It folds easily into their pocket for their next meeting, discussion, or conversation. Imagine your leadership coming to you for the answers. They come in with their question, and they leave with their answer in hand, efficiently and effectively. Additionally, they may ask you to send them the information electronically. No problem! You already know the page and the document and can easily oblige.

The notebook also contains references to changes that are being considered, such as notes in the margins, highlights for key points, and Post-it flags for items needed. When the annual review of policies rolls around, it is easy to pull the notebook and see what changes were identified that can be made.

Additionally, your Handy Dandy Notebook serves as a reminder to your staff that the first step when asking a question should be "Look at what the policy says." It is great that you know the answers; it is better to teach others how to find their own answers.

"If you give a man a fish, you feed him for a day. If you teach a man to fish, you feed him for a lifetime."

Lao Tzu

If you always provide the answers to your team, they will always come to you for those answers. When they are equipped with their own Handy Dandy Notebook and can find the answers themselves, time is saved on both ends. They also gain confidence in themselves and their ability to execute their duties and the boundaries in which to do them. Empower your team to create their own notebooks/resource guide of the rules. Show them where the policies, procedures, regulations, and reference materials they may need are kept. Task them with organizing their own version of a notebook/resource guide, keeping in mind they will be required to reference it while performing their duties. That way, when they come to you with a question you know can be found in a policy, you can simply ask, "What does the policy say?"

I feel like my role as a leader is to teach and empower my team so they do not need me. My goal is to work myself out of a job. With that in mind, think of what a gift it would be to walk into a leadership position and the previous leader left you their Handy Dandy Notebook? It would be like finding a treasure map with all the pitfalls and dangerous areas outlined. Talk about leaving something better than you found it!

How to Approach Changes

Okay, you know what the rules are now. You may want to jump in and start making changes. Your team may have a mountain of pebbles and boulders they are testing you on and pushing you to address. It is tempting to just make changes, win them over, and get this ball rolling. Stop! You may see so many things that need to be adjusted already. It is tempting to start now; I urge you to refrain. There are a couple of things you need to do before you begin the overhaul.

First, build trust. Huh? We are talking about rules, and we are jumping into trust building? Yes, build trust.

The team you are now leading is in a transition phase. They have lost their previous leader whom they knew well, and now they are uncertain of what you are going to do. Perhaps they do not know you, or they do not trust you yet. Perhaps you moved from a co-worker to a leader role on the same team. They do not know how you will be as a leader. Anything you implement could be seen as a threat to the culture, the team, or their livelihood. They are leery of your motives.

Do not take it personally. Give them time and opportunity to trust you. How?

Pebbles! No, not Fred and Wilma's daughter on *The Flintstones*. Pebbles, as in those little rocks we mentioned in Chapter 2. Your team has pebbles in their shoes. Not literally, but they have small things getting in the way of doing their jobs as efficiently as possible. Ask them what their pebbles are and then remove the pebbles!

Why exactly is this pebbles bit in the middle of the rules chapter? Because you cannot make any changes, aka remove any pebbles, if you do not know whether the rules around the pebble are red or blue.

Remember: Red = cannot change the rule; Blue = possible to change the rule. Find out the pebble, and research the rules to see if the pebble can be eliminated, moved, or modified.

When you solve small issues based on their ideas and feedback, making it easier to do their jobs — well, that is how you build trust.

Pebble-and-Rock Strategy

When I first began working with a different company with a team who had suddenly lost their previous boss, I set up a standing weekly meeting. One agenda item was: Pebbles and Rocks. First, I asked them what the pebbles in their shoes were and how they thought they could be removed. During the week, I would work on how to remove the pebble. At next week's meeting, I gave an update on the pebbles. Slowly, the pebble list decreased, and trust began building.

To prevent the meeting from turning into a gripe session, I also paired Pebbles with Rocks. I asked who "rocks" on the team. This allowed them to give kudos to each other or other departments. This process helps others recognize the team's contributions and instills a sense of pride in their work. Recall that psychological contract from Chapter 2 and the why or purpose part? When an employee knows their efforts are contributing to something bigger than themselves and it is recognized by their team as good, they will strive to keep producing quality work. Imagine having a team in which each member is performing their best, contributing to the purpose, and performing consistently. That is the type of team and culture needed to do great work.

The next step before implementing big or boulder-sized changes: get people's input. Through the pebbles process, you are going to learn where major changes can be made. When the pebbles add up to boulder-sized issues, the sphere of input will increase as well to include other teams, departments, and leaders whose processes may be affected by a large overhaul by your team.

One boulder-sized improvement was replacing an outdated software system. This software basically stored data. It has some canned reports, several of which no longer worked. I knew this had to be changed. Yet to several of the staff and IT, there was a love and loyalty to this software. This was a boulder to overcome, and it was not going to happen quickly.

I started with asking what the process was to propose new software. My journey to find software to meet all of our department's needs quickly began and turned into a full-blown project with an official

Project Manager. The project management approach ensured all the details were addressed, relevant departments included for input, and processes outlined for a successful implementation. The new software was implemented about three years after that original inquiry on how to propose new software.

To say the new software revolutionized our work processes would be an understatement. Although tackling this boulder took years, the trust it built within our team and the other involved departments was paramount.

Gather Wisdom from the Team

As that trust is built, your staff will tell you about their ideas for improvements. When there is an idea for change, talk it out with your team. You may choose a few key members if you have a large team. That is fine. You want their input, opinion, and expertise so you can leverage their knowledge before you make the final decision and plan.

When you do not ask, you might take a path that causes more problems or has a less than desirable result. Here is an example:

One morning when I was around ten years old, I woke up before everyone else. To surprise my family, I decided to make pancakes. We had the Bisquick baking mix which listed the additional main ingredients needed to make pancakes: milk and eggs. Looking in the kitchen, I realized we had no eggs.

No problem, I thought. *Mayonnaise has eggs in it.* So I used mayonnaise instead of eggs. Then I found we had no milk. *No problem.* We had Milnot, which was sort of like milk, so I used Milnot.

I whipped up a batch of pancakes, fully confident about my substitution choices, and had them ready when my family got up. They hungrily dug into breakfast and their faces turned awful sour very quickly. Mom asked, "Honey, what did you put in these?"

I proudly rattled off my genius substitutions while the whole family spat out what they had begun chewing. If only I had consulted someone with a little experience in the kitchen, I would have known that my genius substitutions would not work.

When people have an opportunity to think it through, give input, and ask questions, they are more likely to support the change. Having the support of those affected by change is key to successful transformations in the workplace. And you could save some time and heartache from making a bad batch of pancakes in the process.

Additional Reading List

The 21 Irrefutable Laws of Leadership – John Maxwell
Business Made Simple – Donald Miller

Who Moved My Cheese? – Spencer Johnson, MD

Your Next Steps

1. Identify the Red Rules for your company, industry, field.

2. Gather documentation of the policies, procedures, bylaws, reference materials that already exist that pertain to your team and responsibilities.

3. Organize the documentation so you can easily access and search it in the future. This can be electronic or printed.

4. Begin a list of possible pebbles and boulders and keep adding to it as you and your team come across issues to be addressed.

Bonus Tip: If you want to look brilliant, title the name of the running issues list "Possible

Performance Improvement Projects." Then you look like you are always looking at ways to improve; and it sounds better than "Stuff that needs fixed" list.

Chapter 4
Know How to Communicate

Communication is not easy! It is learned over time, with much practice. As a leader you will deliver various types of messages, in numerous ways, and likely repeatedly. In order to effectively inform your team of deadlines, projects, ideas, or elicit their ideas, pebbles, and boulders, you must learn how to communicate. There are the easy and fun communications like telling someone they are being promoted or getting a raise. There are mundane reminders of what is happening this week, what the priorities are, trainings and the like. And then there is the delivering of a difficult message, with grace, truth, and consequences — which is tough. Regardless of the type of message being delivered, it takes thought, practice, and consistency to be an effective communicator.

Communication and Feelings

One definition of communication from the *New Oxford American Dictionary* is "the successful conveying or sharing of ideas and feelings." Oh boy, feelings?! Yes, we must learn how to successfully convey ideas and feelings. You might think, "Why? This is business; feelings have no part." This thinking could not be further from the truth.

People can be, and are, motivated by their emotions. The feeling of excitement may motivate one to work faster or more efficiently, while a sense of dread may negatively affect productivity. If you want a productive and cohesive team, insight on how people tick, their motivators, how they communicate, and how they react (feel) is essential.

I am going to be vulnerable here and share a secret weakness of mine: I am very confident on the outside, yet I can question my self-worth, a lot. When my boss needs to communicate with me on something that did not go quite right, I will have different responses based on how the communication is delivered.

For example, if my boss says, "I just cannot believe you let this happen. This is a mess. What are you going to do to fix this?" I immediately believe that internal fear about my self-worth is true — and I shut down. I will then beat myself up more than my boss ever could. I will contemplate if I am even capable of doing my job, and I will be highly unlikely to come up with a good solution to the issue at hand.

On the other hand, if my boss says, "You are valuable to this team. However, an issue has occurred, and we need to figure out how to fix it." I am all in! Let us get it fixed. And I will likely admit to my faults during the conversation.

Learn to understand people and how they are wired. This helps you to deliver information in a way they can receive it, understand it, and be appropriately motivated to act upon it. To say it plainly, it is not just about the message. The delivery is key.

Courage in Conflict

Author Patrick Lencioni talks about three types of courage in episode 176 of the *At the Table with Patrick Lencioni Podcast*:

    1. Public – The willingness to stand up and make a public statement even when you

know there is risk involved.

2. Interpersonal – Having a difficult conversation with one or two people in a room where there is confrontation, and you might not be popular or well-liked in that moment.

3. Self – The courage to confront yourself about what is true, even when it is difficult to face the truth.

To communicate well, you need courage to self-reflect; to make improvements to your style and method; to have difficult, awkward, or uncomfortable conversations; and to stand in front of a group and deliver a message or take a stand.

I recall one particularly difficult conversation — one of those confrontational, uncomfortable, hard conversations with a team member. I leaned on my Human Resources department to ensure I was using the right policy, form, language, and process. Even with all the preparation, it was not easy. The team member was an employee who I knew did not accept feedback well. The conversation was necessary in order to bring light to an issue and hopefully guide this team member to self-evaluation, and reflection, and ultimately improvements.

Were either of us happy once the discussion was over? Hardly! The team member reacted as anticipated based on previous conversations. I was thankful I survived that conversation, but knew there would be more to come in the near future. Yes, feelings are a factor when communicating; sometimes those emotions are not positive. You still must have the courage to have the conversation, even when it is difficult.

Constructive Conflict

There will be conflict, whether it be in a difficult one-on-one discussion or as a team discusses issues or ideas. Patrick Lencioni, in his book *The Advantage*, talks about the conflict continuum. A team with no conflict is living at one end of the continuum in artificial harmony; it is not real harmony because no one is speaking up about issues that need to be addressed. On the opposite end, there is a team full of mean-spirited personal attacks where no issues are solved or addressed. Although the teams on each end of the spectrum seem different, they are both failing to make any progress addressing any issues, pebble or boulder sized.

Somewhere in the middle is the ideal conflict point, where between artificial harmony and the middle you find constructive conflict. Constructive conflict is where ideas are discussed, and innovation and change can take place without personal attacks. *Ideas* are discussed, not people. Then, if you continue too far along the continuum, somewhere between the middle and the mean-spirited attacks, is the destructive conflict. This is where *people* are discussed, blame is cast, and no innovation happens. The conflict we want to strive for having on our team is the constructive conflict. When a team has this healthy constructive conflict, the pebbles and boulders can be discussed openly, solutions begin to develop, and collaboration within the team increases.

Craft the Message

After reading those last two paragraphs, which end of the spectrum do you believe your team to be on? Take that into consideration when developing or crafting a message; think about the emotion that would be best elicited from this communication. Do you need to challenge the artificial harmony that exists on your team and get some real discussion going about a new project? Do you need to create buy-in for a new project to circumvent the destructive conflict? Craft and deliver each message so as to create the vision, emotion, and action your team needs to reach the end goal. There is a saying about starting with the end in mind. Start with communication and feelings in mind.

What better example of starting with the end in mind is there than the first day on a new job? Crafting a message for that first encounter with your team can be intimidating; you know the emotions you want to create and the fears you want to calm; yet you may not know the team culture. It was my first meeting, on day one with my new team. We gathered together in a conference room, and I asked each of them to tell me about themselves: Name, longevity at the company, and their role on the team. When it got to me (last), I told them my background, very quickly, not lengthy. I spent more time conveying how excited I was to get to know them, work *with* them (I rarely say someone works *for* me, as that does not promote teamwork), and learn from them. The goal was to make them excited and look forward to what lies ahead, not dread what the new boss is going to change, be like, or demand.

Of course, messaging is just as important when difficult projects arise, or when serious changes are being made to the workplace. Recall how the software needed to be replaced? The team also had to be sold on the new software. At this point, I knew my team well, where we fell on the spectrum, and software was an essential boulder that had to be dealt with. Knowing these elements, I developed numerous messages to bring the whole team on board with the challenge of changing our software. This process took time, and we eased the introduction slowly into the normal conversations and meetings. I was transparent as to progress, meetings, decisions, and timelines along the way, so there were very few, if any, surprises. I demonstrated the software every chance I got, relating it to their work and processes. I also opened up the floor for questions and involved those who were interested, giving them a sense of ownership. This consistent, open communication eased stress and helped them embrace the changes that were coming.

Where to Begin

You may be thinking, *Great, now I have to know everyone. How am I going to do that by Monday?* You do not have to do this immediately. Usually, teams give a little grace to the new boss, at least for a couple of weeks!

Remember the get to know your team chapter and the one-on-one meetings? What did you glean from those? What motivates your individual team members? Observe their communications with each other. Look at body language; learn to understand the silent signs and signals to evaluate when people are comfortable and uncomfortable.

A really great book on body language is *What Every Body Is Saying* by Joe Navarro. He is an ex-FBI agent with so many stories and insights on reading body language. My favorite is watching people's feet. The feet do not lie. If you are actively mentally engaged in a conversation, your feet will be facing the person you are conversing with. If you are not mentally engaged and are ready to leave the conversation, one or both of your feet will begin to point in a direction away from the person you are conversing with. Pay attention to your own feet the next time you are in a conversation, and see what they are telling about you.

Digging Deeper

It was Easter Sunday, and the family had gathered at one of the cousins' new home. Her two daughters, ages four and six, were giving me the grand tour. In the middle of the tour, the four-year-old looked at me and said, "My sister's brain is different." Surprised by her comment, yet aware of her sister's challenges, I responded with, "Well, God made each of us different."

Although we all know that fundamentally, we are all different, when it comes to communication, we can tend to forget those differences. Or we falsely presume everyone gives and receives information the same way we do. We each receive, evaluate, process, store, retrieve, and provide information in a variety of ways. How we interact with the world and others is based on our personalities as well as what we learned growing up.

Eventually, you will want to invest the time and energy into having your team take a personality test. There are numerous personality and working style tests you and your team can take. A few I have found helpful over the years:

Enneagram – This test gives us insight as to why we are the way we are. There are nine types:

- Type **One** is principled, purposeful, self-controlled, and perfectionistic.

- Type **Two** is generous, demonstrative, people-pleasing, and possessive.

- Type **Three** is adaptable, excelling, driven, and image-conscious.

- Type **Four** is expressive, dramatic, self-absorbed, and temperamental.

- Type **Five** is perceptive, innovative, secretive, and isolated.

- Type **Six** is engaging, responsible, anxious, and suspicious.

- Type **Seven** is spontaneous, versatile, acquisitive, and scattered.

- Type **Eight** is self-confident, decisive, willful, and confrontational.

- Type **Nine** is receptive, reassuring, complacent, and resigned.

You can find out more at
www.enneagraminstitute.com.

Myers Briggs – According to the Myers & Briggs Foundation website's Myer-Briggs® Overview, "The MBTI assessment is designed to help people identify and gain some understanding around how they take in information and make decisions, the patterns of perception and judgment, as seen in normal, healthy behavior."

Find out more at www.themyersbriggs.com and www.myersbriggs.org/my-mbti-personality-type/myers-briggs-overview/.

Working Genius – I have so much to say about this one! *Working Genius* by Patrick Lencioni revolutionized my thought process on problem solving, how work gets done, and the various strengths we each have when it comes to work. The premise is that work gets done through the six phases outlined in the acronym WIDGET.

- Wonder – asking the questions, like why, what if, could this be improved?

- Invention – thinking of possible solutions and answers to the questions.

- Discernment – discerning whether the solutions and answers could actually work.

- Galvanizing – rallying the troops behind an idea, plan, goal.

- Enablement – actually doing the work necessary to accomplish a goal.

- Tenacity – ensuring the finish line is reached.

Of these six phases of work, each person has two that are their genius, two that are competencies, and two that are frustrations. When you are working in your genius, it is like refilling your cup, having the best day ever; you are energized and could do those types of tasks all day long! When working in your competency, you are not necessarily refilled, nor are you drained. Finally, working in your frustration, you are frustrated, totally drained, and left thinking, *please do not make me do that again*!

Find out more at www.workinggenius.com.

Connecting the Dots

How does knowing someone's Enneagram or Working Genius help communication? Let us use my wonderful husband as an example. I refer to my husband's personality and working style as Code Yellow; he is an Enneagram Type Six and has Discernment as one of his Working Geniuses. He is always evaluating what could go wrong, worst-case scenario, what is the exit plan, and on and on. He can often jump to the worst-case scenario before I have even finished the first sentence of my next brilliant idea.

I, on the other hand, am more of a Positive Pollyanna. Things can work out; we can fix it! Let's go for it! For years, I thought he just hated every single one of my ideas as he was always telling me why they would not work, how much it would cost, how badly things could go wrong. I just knew he wanted to squash all my dreams.

And then I began to connect the dots and figured out that he was using his gift of discernment to point out the faults or what-could-go-wrongs in my plans so that I could adjust for them. He was not trying to kill my ideas. He was trying to make them better.

We have learned over 20+ years of marriage how to adjust our communication styles with each other. You do not have 20 years to figure everyone on your team out. You can, however, invest time, energy, and perhaps a little money and choose a personality or working style test for your team members to take. Once everyone has their results, share them. Have a meeting explaining the results and how it relates to working with each other.

Why are communication and learning how others communicate so important? As a leader, you must deliver countless pieces of information to your team *and* ensure they understand it! If they do not understand, they will not act on it. If they do not act on it, the job does not get done. How do you ensure they understand the communication? Repeat yourself. What was that? Repeat yourself.

When I worked at the hospital, I was responsible for delivering various messages to the Medical Staff — meeting reminders, reminders to vote on certain topics, to return their applications, complete their medical records, and so much more. The rule of thumb was to deliver the message seven times in seven different ways. I have since found the rule of seven is a marketing tactic, but it works! You will feel like a broken record, but you will need to repeat key ideas, plans, projects, goals, steps, due dates, and policies three to five times before it will stick with your employees. Keep bringing it up in weekly emails, team meetings, and everyday conversations. Writing it down is helpful especially to refer back to later, when perhaps even you cannot remember all the details.

Making It Personal

People long to be heard and known. Once you understand how someone is wired, how they best receive communication, and their drive, you can tailor the message and the delivery to them. When it clicks, they feel heard and known. And this makes them feel valued. When they feel valued, they often give it their all.

Learning personality traits is not where communication development ends. Continue learning by listening and observing your teammates. Then, continue to practice active listening. The art of active listening can be a challenge. I tend to always have a story; I know you are shocked. To ensure I listen actively, I take notes, especially if a story or other idea comes to mind; I can write it down and not interrupt the person speaking. Through the practice of active listening, you glean the emotions of the speaker and often the reasons behind those emotions.

Think of it like putting together a puzzle. Each conversation you have with someone gives you a little bit better picture of them as a whole person. When you can understand the whole person, you are able to understand their emotions and reactions. This understanding is part of what is known as Emotional Intelligence.

Emotional Intelligence is knowing how to manage your own emotions and understand the emotions of others. The five elements to emotional intelligence are: self-awareness, self-regulation, motivation, empathy, and social skills. Like the difficult conversation example from earlier, I could not control how the employee was going to react. However, knowing how they are wired, I could identify the emotions behind their behavior. This helped me have a better understanding of where they came from and how to tailor my interaction with them. Reading *Emotional Intelligence 2.0* is an excellent way to identify areas where you can grow your Emotional Intelligence to increase your communication and conflict management skills.

Communication at All Levels

As a leader within an organization, communication is going to occur at multiple levels. You will need to use your skills to communicate above your level and across your level. Understanding what can and should be shared at various levels of your organization is important. Refer back to knowing the rules. Is some information considered confidential? Protected by laws or regulations? Know these rules before relaying something you cannot take back.

OATH

No, you may not be a judge or government official sworn into office, but you can use an OATH to help filter and craft your communication.

- **O**pen – Provide as much information as appropriate and allowable for the situation.

- **A**ccurate – It seems obvious to not provide false information; yet situations arise when not all facts are available yet. Share what is accurate and not what is supposed. Ensure you know the rules, processes, standards, and laws around the topic you are communicating.

- **T**imely – You must balance having the details and accuracy with how timely the communication needs to happen.

- **H**onest – Your team (at each level of the organization) are looking for your honest take on the situation. Not brutal honesty, but respectful and professional honesty is helpful.

James Humes said, "The art of communication is the language of leadership." As you continue to develop skills to understand people and increase your emotional intelligence, your ability to create meaningful and impactful communication will grow — thus allowing your team to work together efficiently and effectively toward the unified goal.

Additional Reading List

How to Win Friends and Influence People – Dale Carnegie

The 6 Types of Working Genius – Patrick Lencioni

The Advantage – Patrick Lencioni

What Every Body Is Saying – Joe Navarro

Leadership Conversations: Challenging High-Potential Managers to Become Great Leaders – Alan S. Berson and Richard G. Stieglitz

Emotional Intelligence 2.0 – Travis Bradberry and Jean Greaves

<u>Your Next Steps</u>

1. Review the notes you took from your one-on-one meetings with your direct reports. What can you glean regarding personality and communication preferences from your notes?

2. Identify a personality test to take with your team. Check with your Human Resources Department to determine if they have

resources you are able to use.

3. Once identified, take the test along with your team and schedule a meeting to review the results.

Chapter 5
Know Your Role and Expectations

Take care of your team and clear the path for them to be able to do their jobs well. That is your main responsibility in its simplest form. Your job description, however, does not say that. The policies, procedures, laws, and accreditation standards do not say that either. Policies, procedures, laws, and accreditation standards all outline the boundaries in which the company and you are to operate and function.

My first week on the job as the Interim Director at the hospital was eye-opening! Going from an employee to a management position has a whole new set of expectations and tasks. For example:

- Timecards – Yes, people really do expect a paycheck, and those do not just magically get approved and generated by Human Resources or Payroll.

- Reports – Who knew there were so many people needing to know so much information about the work our team was doing?

- Meetings – Seriously, why are there so many meetings? Do people not know there is work to be done?

- Chief Problem Solver – I was now expected to solve all the problems, including but not limited to the bathroom not working, printer not working, and even, *this person is eating a whole rotisserie chicken at her desk, and I am going to throw up or quit if you do not fix it!* (Yes, that really happened.)

- Personnel – There is a lot here, including learning to interview, hiring, documenting incidents and issues before they become a full-blown problem, firing, coaching, writing and giving performance evaluations, giving raises, and justifying why there is a need to hire for a refill or new position.

- Special Projects – On the job description, the phrase "other duties as assigned" is code for special projects. You will be in charge of so many unique projects, like new software, new regulations, performance improvement projects, and collaboration with other departments and teams.

- Organizational level thinking – Each level of leadership has a different level of thinking. For example, the CEO level of thinking is not the day-to-day operations; it is future level thinking, planning, and anticipating where the industry is and where it is going. By comparison, the supervisor level thinking is problem-solving today's issues in order to ensure the work gets done this week.

More Than the Job Description

The list above is probably vaguely referenced in your job description with a few "provides oversight," "monitor," and "ensure" phrases thrown in with some generalized language. How do you know the actual day-to-day, must-get-done items for you and your team? When learning about the rules, you began to become familiar with the tasks, functions, and job duties for which you and your team are responsible. Grab that Handy Dandy Notebook, go through those regulations, policies, and standards, and note the tasks that must occur to ensure compliance. While noting all the tasks, include the timeframes and deadlines for them to be completed.

You may be realizing that I am a stickler for documenting, so this next suggestion may come as no surprise: document the tasks and deadlines into a spreadsheet or an electronic document. Voilà, you now have a specific list of responsibilities for you and your team to ensure are completed.

This exercise also helps connect the red rules to the work being done; use that spreadsheet and add a column for the Red Rules and note them as you go along. Armed with the spreadsheet and knowledge of the rules, you will better understand what can and cannot be changed, modified, or deleted all together.

What Is It You Do?

Consider logging all of the tasks you are responsible for, when they are due along with frequency, collaborators in the process, the red rules (remember the regulatory requirements), and where the instructions (procedures) are located. Continue updating the log, and it can end up serving multiple purposes like:

- Proof you need a raise due to increased job duties.

- Figuring out if the tasks constitute more than 1 FTE (full time employee) and serving as documentation to support your request for an additional employee.

- A list of tasks that could be delegated.

- A roadmap of what needs to be done if you are not available due to extended leave, sickness, or when you get that new promotion and one of your amazingly trained and equipped team members gets promoted to your old position!

But Wait, There Is More

Just like any great infomercial, *there is still more*: the expectations from your leadership. Everyone leads differently, yet we sometimes think we all are the same. Everyone has a different idea of what they expect from their team. To have a clear understanding of what is expected of you, you must have a conversation. Time to use those communication skills!

Ask for a meeting with your boss and whomever else you have found that you report to and ask specific questions. Here are some starter questions:

- What is the reporting structure?

- Are there specific tasks not outlined in your job description they expect from you?

- How often do they want reports and updates? And in what format do they prefer communication (email, chat, text, phone call, face-to-face meeting)?

- Are there any problem areas on your team you need to know about? If so, have there been any attempts to fix them?

- What resources should you know about?
- What reoccurring deadlines, meetings, reports, and the like, do you need to know about?

- Is there anything else they would like you to know or tell you about?

There may also be instances where you report to an additional leader(s). Perhaps you provide oversight for more than one area, and each area reports up through a different executive. Maybe there is a dotted line between you and another leader in the organizational chart that requires you to report to more than one person.

Remember the story about the residency program and balancing between the hospital administration and the Medical Staff? The Director position I was in answered to both administration and the Medical Staff. The same expectations meeting can and should occur with them to ensure you know your role, what they need from you, and what they expect from you.

The Boss's Boundaries

During those expectations meetings, the rules or boundaries you are expected to lead within should have begun to emerge. Just like the kids who needed the fence in the playground, you need to know the boundaries in which your boss expects you to operate. For example, do they expect you to review every personnel issue or decision with them before you make it? Do they want to be aware of issues as they occur or once you have resolved them?

When you move from an employee to a leader, you want to learn the boundaries of the new role. When you take a new leadership position, you want to know what the boss's boundaries are, so you do not overstep your authority and end up stepping on the boss's toes.

Rowing

I would like to note how beneficial these expectation conversations can be for your team. Do they know what you expect from them? Do they know what your leaders expects from the team? Setting clear expectations, tasks, and goals helps point the team in the same direction. Patrick Lencioni says it this way in *The Five Dysfunctions of a Team*, "If you could get all the people in the organization rowing in the same direction, you could dominate any industry, in any market, against any competition, at any time."

Have you read the book or watched the movie *The Boys in the Boat*? It is about a junior rowing team that won at the 1936 Olympics. When they were focused on the same goal, knew their part in getting to the goal, and executed within the boundaries of their position, they won! An essential part of your job as a leader is to ensure the members of your team know the expectations, their roles and responsibilities, and the boundaries in which they can perform, so they can all row in the same direction.

Maybe you have never had an expectations conversation before, or it has been a while. This is something you can do anytime, especially if there have been large organizational upheavals, your boss is new, or it just feels like something is off.

Prioritization

By now, you may start feeling a skosh overwhelmed; that task list grew a lot with that last exercise. Stop for a second and inhale. Now, exhale. First, remember there is a team you are leading whose job is to help you execute the items on that long to-do list. Additionally, there are some prioritization tools that can help you manage your time. For the rest of this chapter, we are going to explore saying yes, prioritizing, and running your day.

Evaluate Your Yes

I have an issue with rarely saying no when asked to do something, start something, take on another project, and be involved. I love helping! However, I hate my schedule when I say yes to everything. When saying yes to something, we are saying no to something else at the same time.

I had an opportunity to join another women's group at church. I already knew these women. I loved spending time with them. The new group would be reading books together, another favorite thing of mine. Oh, how I wanted to say yes to the invitation! Then I recalled hearing the advice that saying yes to one thing meant saying no to another. The idea behind it is we only have so much time in a day. Saying yes to a time commitment means not spending that time doing something else.

I stopped and considered what I would be saying no to if I was saying yes to a new group that was meeting every other Monday night. At the time my husband and I had two teenagers, fourteen and seventeen years old. Our 17-year-old was a senior in high school and worked her part-time job Thursday through Sunday evenings. Between her schedule and the commitments I already had, we could only have dinner as a family on Mondays and Tuesdays.

Considering she was a senior in high school, and she was planning on moving out the next summer, I calculated we only had 104 family dinner opportunities before she was to graduate. Talk about perspective! It was easy to say no to the new women's group invite because I knew what it meant I was saying no to.

As a new boss, you will need to evaluate your yeses and nos. They not only affect your time but also the resources of your team. When considering projects, does your team have the margin to take on another project? Consider budget, time, material, training, expertise, and so forth.

Right, like we can say no to our boss. Who has that luxury? If you are not at the top of the leadership chain, you may feel like you always have to say yes. Here is where the phrase "yes, and" can be helpful. Perhaps the answer is "**yes**, we or I can take that on, **and** we will need XX amount of overtime, these resources, and so on, to be able to accomplish it and keep up with current workload." Or perhaps "**yes**, that can be accomplished, **and** what can be put on the back burner or removed from the workload in order to be successful?"

Remember, taking on more (saying yes) only to sacrifice the team's morale, productivity, personal balance, or your own morale, productivity, or personal balance is only a setup for more work and faster burnout. Practice and learn the art of evaluating your yes before giving it.

Personal Priority Pyramid

Several years ago, I came across the concept of a personal priority pyramid, which is another way of evaluating your yes. I tend to struggle with trying to do all the things all the time and sometimes simultaneously. At the time I learned this concept, a heaviness was on me, and I honestly felt like I was failing at all of my responsibilities — parenting, leading, serving, resting, working, friending, and spousing. Then I read that not every task we have for ourselves has the same weight. In other words, not everything we do is on the same priority level. Our personal prioritization system should be more like a pyramid than a straight line. Your priority pyramid helps you determine what is a priority based on the life you want to have.

My mouth dropped, and I just sat there re-reading this idea that we should not assign every area of our lives the same level of importance. What a concept; but wait, there was more! Once this personal priority pyramid was developed, I could use it to make decisions about my time and energy and then not feel guilty about choosing between conflicting tasks, meetings, appearances, and the like. *Yes, please tell me how*, I thought.

The first step is to make a list of your priorities. For example: self-care, family, work, church/ faith. Next, put them in order of importance to you in this season of life. Priorities change from time to time, depending on your current goals or the season of life you are in. Currently, I have a goal to write this book. Which means that I have placed my writing into my pyramid.

My normal importance order is family, self-care, church/faith, and work. During this season of writing, I have inserted writing between family and self-care. Putting all of this into a pyramid, it would look like the top layer would be family, next layer writing, the next layer self-care, next layer church/ faith, then the bottom layer work. This pyramid represents what I have determined is important in my life and is my pre-decision of how I choose to spend my time and energy.

Now, how do I use this pyramid to make decisions? Recall that I tend to do all the things all the time and at the same time. Which means, I could have a work dinner that conflicts with my women's group. Which do I choose so that I do not feel guilty? Look at my pyramid; church/faith is higher on the pyramid than work. When building the pyramid, I determined that church/faith takes precedence over work. So when choosing between women's group and work dinner, women's group is the choice based on my current priorities.

Okay, here is one more personal example. I would really like to sit on the couch right now and just veg out and watch a movie and relax. However, I have a deadline to complete this chapter. Consulting my pyramid, writing comes before self-care (aka, vegging out on the couch on a Saturday afternoon); and instead I am keeping to my priorities and finishing this chapter.

The decisions we make consistently (good, bad, wise, or not so wise) culminate into the life we live. At the end of my life, I want to be the woman who went for her dreams, spent time with her family and friends, and shared God's love with others. I would rather not be known as a couch potato.

Running Your Day

Jim Rohn says, "Either you run the day or the day runs you." Being a leader comes with lots of people, tasks, meetings, projects, problems, lunches, and new ideas all vying for your time. Numerous requests flood in, and you are trying to evaluate your yes. If you are simply responding and reacting, you will be exhausted because the day ran you. Instead, you need to run your day by planning.

The process of running your day begins by looking at the wide angle, your year. Why the year? Because days turn into weeks, weeks into months, months into years, years into decades, and decades into a lifetime. What are the big personal things (things at the top of your pyramid) that need to be carved out on your calendar? Anniversaries, birthdays, vacations, conferences, and holidays are all things that could be important to you and should be scheduled into your calendar as early as possible. These are going to be your non-negotiable dates that you are prioritizing in your life and your schedule.

All right, your personal big priorities are on the calendar. It would make sense to move onto the work priorities; however, I have one more personal priority suggestion: lunch. This year I did something different, and I scheduled a lunch meeting with myself from 11 a.m. to 1 p.m. every day. I do not take two-hour lunches, but before I began reserving time on my daily calendar for lunch, I was rarely leaving my desk for a break or for lunch. Now, I get a half-hour to an hour lunch break where I can actually eat, and not at my desk while working. The other hour that is blocked, I use for catching up or working on other important tasks. This is a new practice I will be doing every year from now on as it has reduced my stress, increased my productivity, and helped me take a break and take care of me each day.

Now it is time to look at the big work priorities. Is there a project that will take a substantial amount of time? Schedule blocks of time to work on the project leading up to the deadline. Just like your personal priorities change and have seasons, so do your work priorities. Let's look at how to prioritize the work to-do list.

The Eisenhower Matrix is a task management tool that helps organize tasks between urgent and important tasks so you can figure out what needs to be worked on immediately, what can be scheduled, what can be delegated to someone else, and what can be possibly deleted. Go through that to-do list and determine whether each item is urgent or not urgent, and whether each item is important or not important. This helps you categorize them as follows:

- Urgent and Important – Needs to be done; work on it.

- Not Urgent and Important – Needs to be done but can be scheduled to be worked on.

- Urgent and Not Important – Can be delegated to someone else to complete.

- Not Urgent and Not Important – Consider whether this task is necessary and could it be deleted from the to-do list.

Equipped with your work prioritization, you can now schedule the tasks that need to be completed each day. Remember the goal is to run your day; do so by outlining when you will work on certain tasks.

Here is how I do it; I print my calendar each day. Outlook has a daily print version that divides the day into thirty-minute increments and fills in the meetings already scheduled on my calendar. I then review my to-do list and write in when I will work on certain tasks.

There are always interruptions throughout the day: phone calls, urgent chats, or someone popping into the office. When we are interrupted, it takes roughly twenty minutes to get back into the zone of whatever we were working on before we were interrupted. Sometimes I cannot even remember what I was working on. That is where I can consult my schedule and see what time it is and what I should be working on. For situations when I need uninterrupted time, I shut the door to my office.

Using the methods above of evaluating your yes, prioritizing both personal and work tasks, and scheduling your day so you are running the day, you can turn your to-do list into your done list.

Additional Reading List

The Ideal Team Player – Patrick Lencioni

Leaders Eat Last – Simon Sinek

Leadership Conversations – Alan S. Berson and Richard G. Stieglitz – Chapter 16 – "Develop Your Judgment Gene"

Your Next Steps

1. Construct your personal priority pyramid.

2. Schedule your big personal priorities on your calendar: vacations, birthdays, anniversaries, holidays. Do not forget lunch!

3. Schedule an expectations meeting with your boss. If you already have a standing meeting

with your boss, outline specific questions to ask at your next meeting. This will allow you to get clear direction on their expectations.

Chapter 6

Execute with Confidence and Precision

You have learned about your team. You studied the rules and gleaned the tasks to be done. You keep learning how to tailor communications and deliver messages. Your next step is to put the right people in the right seats on your bus. Jim Collins, in his book *Good to Great*, explains the bus concept.

> First Who, Then What — get the right people on the bus.... Those who build great organizations make sure they have the right people on the bus and the right people in the key seats before they figure out where to drive the bus. They always think first about who and then about what. When facing chaos and uncertainty, and you cannot possibly

predict what is coming around the corner, your best "strategy" is to have a busload of people who can adapt to and perform brilliantly no matter what comes next. Great vision without great people is irrelevant.[2]

You may not always have the ability to hire a whole new team; many times you inherit your team. So how do you go about rearranging seat assignments? You put the puzzle pieces together:

1. Review your notes about each person's strengths and geniuses.

2. What do they like best and least about their current role?

3. What work needs to be done that fits within their strengths, geniuses, and favorite parts of their job?

This is not to say that people will never have to do something that is challenging or something they do not enjoy doing. However, the majority of their

---

2 Jim Collins, "First Who, Then What," Excerpts *from Good to Great*, www.jimcollins.com.

job should not be comprised of tasks and duties that absolutely drain them. When people are doing work that refills them, ignites the passion inside them, and flames their desire to work, they will do more and go farther than you can push them. Their job satisfaction increases, which leads to increased retention rates.

Conversely, if people must do something that frustrates them or drains them the majority of the time, that can lead to quiet quitting. The act of quiet quitting is essentially doing the bare minimum in order to keep your job. Think of the thing you currently dread doing at work. Now, imagine that every day you had to do that task most of the day. How long do you think it would take before you started looking for a new job? Do you think you would perform that task to the absolute best of your ability?

What exactly does this look like? Here are some examples.

- Meeting minutes – Do you have someone who loves writing? Or is great at notetaking? Has an attention to detail? Maybe they are a great fit for minute taking and transcribing.

- Meeting preparations – Perhaps someone on your team is highly organized; they are likely suited to handle meeting preparation and scheduling.

- Celebrations – Is there a party planner extraordinaire on your team? Ask them if they would schedule the celebrations on your team like monthly birthday luncheons and holiday parties.

- Policy reviews – It may sound odd, but some people actually like to review and revise policies. Assigning them the task of policy upkeep can alleviate your stress and bring them increased job satisfaction.

When you are equipped with the knowledge and information on your team's strengths, skills, and geniuses, and pair them with the tasks that need to be done, you are putting the right person in the right seat on your bus. The to-do list gets done with passion and excellence. Now, that is a team that can push the boundaries of what seems to be impossible.

Removing Passengers from the Bus

In *Good to Great*, Jim Collins also explains that having the right people on the bus, and having moved the wrong people off the bus, leads to having people you do not have to manage. Essentially getting the right people — who fit culturally, are teachable, who buy into the mission of the company, and have a good work ethic — allows you to then focus on managing the processes, not the people.

Recall the boulder-sized issue from Chapter 2 where I lead my team through Patrick Lencioni's *Five Dysfunctions of a Team*? I had difficult conversations with employees addressing behavior and/or productivity. Slowly, each person realized the team dynamic was changing, and the old ways were not acceptable anymore. By the end of that year, several team members moved on from our company.

The team that remained is by far the most trusting, productive, accountable, and caring team I have ever been a part of. This team does not have drama, and the only management I do for them is approving timecards, okaying paid time off, and answering questions on things they are learning. This frees up my time to focus on processes and systems. Those systems and processes not only get the work going and flowing, but they also include checks to ensure work is being done accurately and in a timely fashion.

Ensuring the Work Gets Done

Next, we are going to learn about micromanagement and how to implement the best micromanagement practices. NOT! I am kidding! I am the worst micromanager ever. It actually hurts in my chest when I end up having to micromanage someone through a performance improvement plan.

Micromanagement shows a lack of trust in the employee to do their job. When clear expectations are outlined, communicated, and understood, micromanagement should not be necessary. Following up, however, is necessary; checking in on the quality of work is a must. Asking every five minutes if it is done or checking in every two hours on a report is not a must.

As the tasks are assigned, be sure to agree upon timelines for completion; establish regular check-ins or status updates; ensure you are available for questions, roadblocks, or issues that arise; and confirm how and when the final product will be delivered and reviewed.

There can also be others who can review and evaluate the work. For example, in my team we produce files. Each file is reviewed prior to going to a committee chairman or the full committee for review and decision. I do not personally review all the files produced. Our team has a weekly audit on Wednesdays. Each employee is assigned to another employee to review their files. Only those who are trained to produce files can audit files. Each week, anywhere from 50 to 100 files are reviewed. Our committee meets monthly with roughly 400 audited files going each month. If I was the only one auditing, that is all I would do every day, all week, all month... Not an option!

Set up ways to ensure work is completed, timely and accurately. Your team has ideas on how to improve processes; you simply need to ask them.

Check in With Your Team

Patrick Lencioni's book *Death by Meeting* is hilariously and accurately named. No one wants another meeting. However, I have found it extremely beneficial to have one-on-one meetings on a monthly basis with each of my direct reports. In these regular meetings, my staff and I meet and review the following questions. Yes, the same questions every time. You will find that some of your team will prepare their responses and ideas and really take ownership of this dedicated time with you each month.

1. What is going well?

2. Do you have the tools and resources you need to do your job?

3. Do you see any opportunities for improvement and suggestions on how to improve? (Note: this is improvement with processes within the team, the work being done, and can include culture, drama, and so on. This is them keying you into things you may or may not know about, but you need to address.)

4. Is there anybody I should be recognizing and why? (Great things happen and you may not always see them. This helps you give kudos and recognition to others.)

5. Is there anything I or the leadership team can do better to support you?

6. Is there anything else you want me to know or tell me about? (Remember the judge in the Olympic coach trial in Chapter 2? This is a similar question with the same principle. You are going to find out what is important to them, and what is weighing on them.)

Keep a log of their responses and follow up. If they reveal they need a new keyboard, evaluate and take action to ensure they get a keyboard. If they have an idea for improvement that is plausible, see if it can be implemented. You could even give them the authority to implement it. Relay the kudos they gave to the person, department, or team they recognized. Do not let the intel gathered in the one-on-one sit and collect dust. Use it! If you do not use it or act upon it, they will stop sharing the ideas, needs, thoughts, and kudos because they see no action or result.

Being realistic, we know that not all things are possible. That is okay. Be sure to follow up and let them know the outcome, good or not so great. The fact that their idea or feedback was heard and thoughtfully considered goes a long way. The key is to act on the information and close the loop by reporting back to your direct report.

Many companies require employees to have annual goals that are tied to their performance evaluations. They are assigned at the beginning of the year and forgotten within a few months, until the last quarter comes along. Then it is a rushed frenzy to try to complete a year's worth of goals in three months. To ensure your team does not lose sight of those goals, consider adding them as part of your monthly check-in agenda. That way, you can help remind them of their goals without micromanaging, support them along the way, and celebrate when goals are accomplished before the end of the year.

Open Door Policy

You want your team to be able to come to you with issues, solutions, concerns, good catches, and successes. Having an open-door policy is the best way I know of to be available and inviting to your team. Yet, it can become difficult to get your own duties accomplished if there is a revolving door to your office.

Years ago, I developed a scheduled open-door time. I set aside one-to-two-hour blocks of time two to three days a week where my staff could come to me with anything they needed to discuss. They figured out the answers to simple questions on their own while waiting for an open-door time. Additionally, they were able to research and come better prepared to open-door meetings. To top it off, I had more focused time for my duties. Win-win!

Investing in Education

Reading this book is an investment in yourself. Congratulations! We never stop learning and growing. Keep going!

On that first Monday when I was asked to step in as Interim Director at the hospital, it hit me: I knew nothing about leadership. Within the first month, our company had an offsite leadership training. I feverishly took notes, made contacts with other leaders within the organization, and began a list of must-read books suggested by others. My leadership journey to invest in myself had begun. I learned the names of John Maxwell, Stephen Covey, and Jim Collins. A few years later, I began listening to the Craig Groeschel Leadership podcast, then the Jeff Brown Read to Lead podcast. Today, I listen to the following podcasts:

- *Read to Lead* – Jeff Brown

- *At the Table* – Patrick Lencioni

- *Working Genius* – Patrick Lencioni

- *Leadership Podcast* – Craig Groeschel

- *It's a Good Life* – Bryan Buffini

- *Business Made Simple* – Donald Miller

- *A Bit of Optimism* – Simon Sinek

You may have noticed at the end of each chapter is a list of books. They are suggestions for digging in deeper to the concepts and ideas presented in each chapter. I have read so many books and listened to thousands of podcasts that the ideas shared in this book have melded together to develop my style of leadership. However, I have been on this journey for over a decade. You may be just beginning! If something intrigues you and you want to dig further, then consider the suggested books and authors at the end of each chapter as a place to continue learning.

Time is fleeting and limited, and you may not feel like there is time to listen to a podcast or an audio book for that matter. Understandable. If it is important to you, you will find the time. Here are some ways I fit in learning.

- Listen while getting ready in the morning.

- During long drives.

- Create a book club with others at work and meet once a month to discuss the book and concepts.

- While doing chores or cooking dinner.

What opportunities do you have in your day or week to spend 20–30 minutes listening or learning?

Audiobooks are a great way to learn. Our brains process so much faster than we can hear and experience information. Listening while doing something else helps my concentration. Now, that something else is not necessarily actual work that requires deep thought and concentration. It is more like cooking dinner, cleaning the house, mowing the yard, and getting ready in the morning.

Accessing audiobooks does not have to cost you anything. There is an app called Libby. It uses your local library card to access all kinds of books. It is like your local library on your phone.

Conferences

Since 2020, travel to conferences slowed and the availability of virtual conferences increased. There are benefits to both. In-person conferences allow connecting and developing professional relationships with others in your industry. Knowing there are others battling or struggling with similar issues brings some relief that it is not just you. This networking can also spark ideas on how to overcome obstacles as well. And let's be honest, it is nice to visit someplace else for a few days. A change of scenery can bring new perspectives.

Virtual conferences have fewer networking opportunities, yet can be full of excellent content. The virtual conferences I have been involved with recently have a pre-recorded session and a live Q&A with the speakers at the end of the day.

As a leader, our job is to grow and empower our teams. Attending a conference together is a great way to do that. Yet, it is not feasible to shut down the team and their work for a week for a conference. Maybe one or two team members can go, but not all can travel at the same time for in-person conferences.

Virtual conferences allow the opportunity for more of your team to attend and learn. You can evaluate which sessions may be beneficial to certain members of your team. Consider the current responsibilities of attendees as well as their professional aspirations to determine which sessions they should attend. Conference sessions on topics related to their current duties or future goals help create intrigue and ideas.

Use a conference room to set up the feed and allow employees to step away from their desk and congregate and concentrate in a session together. At the end of each day or the end of the conference, bring the team together and share what everyone learned. Are there ideas to be explored or implemented? Who will take charge and see it to completion? Empower your staff to try something new. This grows their confidence, abilities, and collaboration.

There may also be webinars, shorter than conferences, maybe only one to two hours. These are also helpful in staying relevant to your industry and can be set up similarly in a conference room. If your team is virtual, you can find ways for everyone to view the webinar and collaborate afterwards virtually.

Teambuilding

Be careful, do not call it teambuilding; they might get jumpy! Many times a team will ask, "Is this one of those trust fall things?" No! I have never put them through that, but it is always a question lurking in the back of the mind.

Building a strong team culture does not happen without some work. Patrick Lencioni's *Five Dysfunctions of a Team* is an excellent resource, and a good read, on how to identify the areas needing attention and specifics on how to improve and develop a team.

Warning: As a leader, it is both exciting and daunting at the same time to take your team through teambuilding exercises. Some employees are more receptive than others. Keep pushing! Peter

Drucker reminds us of the importance of developing a strong culture because "Culture eats strategy for breakfast." If your team cannot get along, you will have strife consistently, productivity and creativity will decline, and turnover will not be good.

Remember, the goal is to get the "right people on the bus, wrong people off the bus." Exercises like teambuilding help you identify those who are not willing to change and those who are all-in to create a great team culture.

Additional Reading List

The Five Dysfunctions of a Team – Patrick Lencioni

The Advantage – Patrick Lencioni

Death by Meeting – Patrick Lencioni

Good to Great – Jim Collins

Built to Last – Jim Collins

<u>Your Next Steps</u>

1. Outline the strengths of each team member and compare the list to their current job duties. Do they line up, or is there some rearrangement that can be done to increase their job satisfaction, quality of work, and productivity?

2. Schedule monthly individual check-ins with your direct reports. Be sure to let them know the questions ahead of time so they are prepared.

3. Identify one conference or webinar that would be beneficial for your team and schedule it.

Chapter 7
Go Forth and Do

Here is where the rubber meets the road. You are equipped with the basics of leadership. You can outline a plan of next steps to take to lead well. This is where you implement the aha moments, the ideas that were sparked, and you go forth and do! It will not be easy; nothing worth doing is ever easy. Do not miss it; leadership is worth doing.

Be Authentic, Not Perfect

Craig Groeschel reminds listeners in each of his leadership podcasts, "People would rather follow a leader who is *always real* than one who is always right." You and I will never be perfect leaders. We will not always have the answers. We will never have all the knowledge. However, that should not stop us from continually trying, collaborating, and learning. When you acknowledge your humanity, you can admit your shortcomings, weaknesses, and faults. This vulnerability helps your team see you not as a dictator, but as part of the team, part of the solution.

Being a great leader does not mean you will be perfect, and your team does not expect you to be. Being a great leader means being authentic and real with your team. They expect you to be consistent, acknowledge your mistakes, hold them and yourself accountable, paint the vision of where the team is headed, and clear the road for them to make progress toward the goals set before them.

Good Leadership

Good leadership inspires others to do their best work, to learn and grow in their roles, and to push themselves to accomplish more professionally. All of this helps to increase job satisfaction, employee retention, and the ability to recruit employees.

In Craig Groeschel's leadership book *It*, when a team or company has *it*, people are drawn to them. As a leader, you want to have *it*. To date, I have had three previous team members leave to pursue other things, and they have come back to work with me. That tells me we have *it*, and we will continue to strive to keep *it*!

Bad Leadership

Bad leadership feels like the opposite of *it*. When a leader is not sharing knowledge, is lording their authority over the heads of their team, and makes everyone miserable on Sunday night because they do not want to go to work on Monday morning, all of that is definitely not *it*. The turnover on teams with a leader like that might be high. The team may not share ideas on how to improve processes, or have high call-in-sick rates, or have complaints to human resources, or no trust exists on the team. Bad leadership drags even the best team down.

Mistakes Will Happen

Remember that leadership is not easy. You will not be perfect. You will make mistakes, not have a conversation in a timely manner or at all, miss opportunities, say things you should have worded differently… The list of possible missteps can go on and on.

The thing is, no one on your team expects perfection. What they do expect is for you to lead well, to provide direction, encouragement when things get rough, stability each day, support to do their jobs well, and to be real with them. When you make a mistake, own it and apologize sincerely. Then get back to leading and taking the next right steps. This is a key difference between bad leaders and good leaders — the willingness to grow and improve.

Remember, you will not have all the answers. You cannot predict every aspect of what is coming with one hundred percent accuracy. You can use the tools you have gained from this book to develop a team that can weather the storms that will come. Use what you have learned and will learn to create a team that will not only survive but also overcome and thrive in challenging times.

Work Yourself Out of a Job

In Chapter 4, we started with the end in mind when crafting messages to our teams. As you move forward in becoming more proficient as a leader and in your duties, you need to keep the end of your time as the leader in mind. I am not insinuating your demise, but rather your succession plan. How do you want to leave your team? My trusted friend Dawn's advice has stuck with me for years, "Leave it on a high note, sister!"

Leadership turnover happens for many reasons: new opportunities, business closing, upper management changes, life changes, and on some occasions an escort leads the way out of the door. My goal is to leave it on a high note, meaning leave the team as equipped as possible to continue the mission without me. Part of that is teaching and delegating tasks to the team. The leader should not be the only one who knows things like:

- Who to call if the company credit card stops working and production comes to a screeching halt because of it.

- What reports are run and for what purpose.

- When standing company meetings are held and who should attend in the leader's absence or unavailability.

- How to run a meeting.

- Who to call if the software stops working.

- What to do if there is a power failure or Microsoft crashes; what the downtime procedures are.

- How to order more envelopes, supplies, and other essentials to keep the work going.

- All the things that employees think just magically happen behind the scenes.

How exactly do you teach, delegate, and empower others with knowledge? Not all at once; you do not want to overwhelm them. Instead, you leave breadcrumbs along the way for them to find their way. The best way I know how is to document, communicate, delegate, and repeat.

Start by creating a procedure on a task that only you know how to do or only you perform. Save this document to a shared folder that your team can access. In your team meetings, communicate to the team where they can find the folder and the types of procedures that are stored there. Keep repeating this documentation and communicating the process until you have all procedures documented. Shoot for a goal of one to two procedures per month so as not to overwhelm yourself or your team all at once.

Next, embrace the efficiency of delegation. There are usually things that you are doing simply because you have always done them or because the previous leader always did them (cutting off the ends of the ham). Re-evaluate if it is something that only you or your position can do. (Do those red rules say it has to be your position that does the task?)

For several years I coordinated all the annual audits our team was required to perform. There were 12 audits and by regulatory requirements (red rules) they had to be performed annually. To say I struggled to get them done on time was an understatement. One year, it came time to report on the timeliness of the audits, and only 50% of them had been performed in a timely fashion. It was a wakeup call for me; I had to ask for help in completing this vital task.

The plan of action to fix the issue was to develop a team of auditors to perform, document, complete, report to Committee, and follow up on these annual audits. I asked my team for volunteers who wanted to learn how to audit. Three ladies stepped up when I asked. We began meeting weekly for one hour to create the tracking tools necessary to keep up with the audits. Once the tools were created, we divided up the audits equally and scheduled when each audit would be performed.

Next, I began teaching them how to do the whole process from reaching out to initiate an audit, performing the audit, documenting the findings, reporting the findings to Committee, and following up once the Committee made their decision. Week after week we met and learned the rules, the documents, the processes. Month after month and audit after audit, they watched me and helped me, then I watched and helped them. Today, two of the ladies are still on the audit team, Rita and Sydney, and now they do not need me. After that first year, the timeliness went from 50% to 92% compliance. There was that one audit that we missed timeliness by only 5 days. When I took the time to delegate to others, they took it further and did it better than I ever could have on my own.

Will Guidara, in *Unreasonable Hospitality*, says, "Refusing to delegate because it might take too long to train someone will only get in the way of your own growth." Choose a task you can delegate to someone else, and train them on how to complete the task using the procedure you already created. The next time it needs to be done, you can stand by and provide oversight. The third time, they can do it on their own and you simply review the results. In time, they will end up doing the task better than you. Delegation has another upside too; it increases the confidence and knowledge of the employee, which leads to increased job satisfaction.

Breadcrumbs and the Big Picture

Keep communicating at the team level to explain the processes that affect them, as well as tying their daily tasks to the mission and purpose. I call this leaving breadcrumbs. This continued communication helps your team know their importance in the success of the work and the company, also known as seeing The Big Picture.

I have lead teams that   have a monthly Committee meeting that occurs the first Friday of each month. This Committee meeting is where the culmination of all the work our team does during the month gets reviewed and approved by the Committee. If we miss reporting an audit that was completed or presenting a policy for review and approval, then we could fail the timeliness requirements. If a file is not audited and does not appear on the reports, then a provider will not be approved by the Committee and will be delayed at least another month. To put it simply, there is no "good enough" when preparing for and finalizing the Committee packet of reports and documents. Precision and excellence are the only option when preparing for Committee, so there is some pressure during the week it takes to prepare.

During that week, Committee Week as we call it, we are all focused on preparing and finalizing files and reports for the Committee. There are several reports run to find any missing information, incorrect dates, or missing audits. We ensure all files are audited, reviewed by the Committee Chairman, and elevated to Department leadership as appropriate. Many details and steps go into preparing for the Friday morning Committee.

There are some Committee Weeks where there seems to be a consistent issue of a wrong date or missing item on the checklist. When these occur, we review them as a team in our weekly meeting. We review the report, how it was built, and what it detects. We review how each completion of a checklist affects whether or not the file shows on the report. As we tie in their steps in processing and auditing a file and how it affects the reports, we are helping to solidify and improve processes, leaving breadcrumbs and painting the Big Picture. Imagine if I were to approach it by telling my team how they keep messing up and asking why they cannot remember to do these simple steps. That approach does not build up the team, nor does it connect their actions to the bigger picture of accurate data and reports to Committee.

There was one Committee Week when I was so ill I could not commute to work, and even working remotely, I could not stay awake all day. Because we held these conversations over and over, my team had enough breadcrumbs and knew the importance of preparing with excellence and precision; they ran the reports and prepared for Committee. When I was able to log on and work in a few hour bursts, I was simply double checking their reports and helping fix any issues they had not yet figured out. They came together as a team to fit all of their pieces together and successfully prepare for Committee Week with very little assistance from me.

As you continue to become more proficient and learn your job, leave the breadcrumbs and paint the Big Picture for your team. When you leave, leave it on a high note with a team equipped to carry on without you and even one or two who can step into your role.

Keep Growing

Sometimes our title and circumstances do not change; we do. It is one of the reasons I love to keep learning, listening, and reading. With each little piece of knowledge, I am transformed bit by bit. The LaShawna that showed up on that Monday at the hospital and was asked to lead could not handle the situations and decisions that current LaShawna handles.

Within the first six months of being the Director at the hospital, I experienced the first resignation threat. This is where the employee believes they are irreplaceable, and if they leave the entire team will fail. So they use their perceived power and threaten to leave unless you do something they want.

Being still so new in my role and considering the person making the threat was the most knowledgeable in a role I did not know anything about, I panicked. I really tried to maintain my poker face in front of the employee as they delivered their demands to me and their manager.

We thanked them for speaking to us and relayed we would take what they had said into consideration. They walked out of the office. I shut the door, and I cried. Full on broke down and sobbed, saying, "What in the world are we going to do?"

Fast-forward to a few years later. Two ladies were having trouble getting along on my team. Snide comments were being made, they were ignoring one another, and they were generally making the office uncomfortable for everyone. The three of us went into the conference room and laid it all out on the table. It was not easy, and at one point I was scared that it might come to blows between them. Yet the issues were resolved, and I did not cry! The tension subsided. Those ladies went on to work many more years together.

Advance again a few more years, and an employee brought to my attention an interaction they felt was uncomfortable. I thanked them for letting me know and outlined the next steps:

- The employee could email or type up their side of the incident, and I would place it in their file.

- I would meet with the other employee to get their side of the interaction and allow them to document their side.

- I would bring all three of us into a room to discuss office expectations and conflict resolution.

Before lunch that day, we had moved through all of the steps, and I typed up my version of what transpired and placed in both employees' files.

These examples illustrate that we continue to develop our leadership muscles and skills as we face the many situations the come with being the boss. We develop into a new boss while often sitting in that same chair.

I pray you will use the five steps in this book to build your foundation of good leadership and implement small changes over time. It is an honor to lead others through the ups and downs that inevitably come along. Together, good leaders and great teams change the world.

New You, Same Chair

Maybe you picked up this book to prepare for your new leadership role. Or maybe you aspire to be a leader one day and want a jumpstart. Or maybe you are a seasoned leader who wants to get back to basics. Something inside or someone suggested you learn what it takes to transform into a leader and become a new boss. So, you took the time and read the book (thanks, by the way!). And tomorrow when you are back at work, that same chair is still there. The difference is what you decide to do with the insights and tools from this book. Will you be the same you who began reading this book? Or will you be the New Boss in your same chair?

Additional Reading List

Unreasonable Hospitality: The Remarkable Power of Giving People More Than They Expect – Will Guidara

<u>Your Next Steps</u>

1. Think of a bad boss you have worked with. List the things that you think made them a bad leader. Thoughtfully consider whether or not you exhibit any of those traits. If you find something you are not proud of, apologize and change.

2. Choose the next leadership book you will read.

3. Go back through the Next Steps in each chapter and address any you may have missed completing.

4. If you found this book helpful, share it with others.

Additional Resources

Below is a consolidated list of the books referenced at the end of the chapters.

Know Your Team

- *It: How Churches and Leaders Can Get It and Keep It* – Craig Groeschel

- *Leadership Secrets of Santa Claus* – Eric Harvey

- *Start with Why* – Simon Sinek

- *The Five Dysfunctions of a Team* – Patrick Lencioni

Know the Rules

- *The 21 Irrefutable Laws of Leadership* – John Maxwell

- *Business Made Simple* – Donald Miller

- *Who Moved My Cheese?* – Spencer Johnson, MD

Know How to Communicate

- *How to Win Friends and Influence People* – Dale Carnegie

- *The 6 Types of Working Genius* – Patrick Lencioni

- *The Advantage* – Patrick Lencioni

- *What Every Body Is Saying* – Joe Navarro

- *Leadership Conversations: Challenging High-Potential Managers to Become Great Leaders* – Alan S. Berson and Richard G. Stieglitz

- *Emotional Intelligence 2.0* – Travis Bradberry and Jean Greaves

Know Your Role and Expectations

- *The Ideal Team Player* – Patrick Lencioni

- *Leaders Eat Last* – Simon Sinek

- *Leadership Conversations* – Alan S. Berson and Richard G. Stieglitz – Chapter 16 – "Develop Your Judgment Gene"

Execute With Confidence and Precision

- *The Five Dysfunctions of a Team* – Patrick Lencioni

- *The Advantage* – Patrick Lencioni

- *Death by Meeting* – Patrick Lencioni

- *Good to Great* – Jim Collins

Go Forth and Do

- *Unreasonable Hospitality: The Remarkable Power of Giving People More Than They Expect* – Will Guidara

About the Author

When LaShawna Brown first jumped into leadership, she realized there was no quick-start guide to success — and there was not time to read every John Maxwell book in a few days. Over the next decade, LaShawna absorbed all she could on leadership from John Maxwell, Jim Collins, Craig Groeschel, Simon Sinek, Brian Buffini, and many others, in order to develop her own caring, detail-oriented, people-focused approach to leading well. LaShawna has led numerous teams and describes her leadership superpower as stepping into a mess and fixing it.

Today, her learning continues as she regularly listens to leadership podcasts, reads several books a year on leadership, mentors other leaders, and volunteers in several leadership roles. Writing a book was never something she thought she would do. Yet a co-worker and friend planted the seed years ago, and it slowly took root. Over the course of a couple of weeks in 2023, several indicators pointed toward writing a book; her husband mentioned it, she felt God prompting her to write a book on leadership, and then her best friend confirmed it — which is how *New Boss, Same Chair* came about. LaShawna loves to help others, make them laugh, and tell stories. She is hopeful that her heart for people comes through in her writing.

Made in the USA
Coppell, TX
13 April 2025

48251942R00079